Report of the Inquiry into Child Abuse in Cleveland 1987

SHORT VERSION EXTRACTED FROM THE COMPLETE TEXT

Presented to Parliament by the Secretary of State for
Social Services by Command of Her Majesty July 1988

LONDON

HER MAJESTY'S STATIONERY OFFICE

Cm 413   £3.00 net

The Right Honourable John Moore, MP
Secretary of State for Social Services

Dear Secretary of State,

   You asked me to inquire into the arrangements for dealing with child abuse in Cleveland since 1 January 1987, including in particular cases of child sexual abuse. I now submit my Report and recommendations.

Yours sincerely,

Elizabeth Butler-Sloss.

Elizabeth Butler-Sloss

6 June 1988.

REPORT OF THE JUDICIAL INQUIRY INTO THE ARRANGEMENTS FOR DEALING WITH SUSPECTED CASES OF CHILD ABUSE IN CLEVELAND SINCE 1 JANUARY 1987

SHORT VERSION

1. Background to the Inquiry

1. On the 9th July 1987, the Secretary of State for Social Services ordered that a Statutory Inquiry should be established under section 84 of the National Health Service Act 1977 and Section 76 of the Child Care Act 1980 to look into the arrangements for dealing with suspected cases of child abuse in Cleveland from the 1st January 1987.

2. The Inquiry was announced by the Minister for Health in the House of Commons on the 9th July 1987 (Hansard Volume 119 number 15 Column 526) and arises from an unprecedented rise in the diagnosis of child sexual abuse during the months of May and June 1987 in the County of Cleveland, principally at Middlesbrough General Hospital. Enormous concern was voiced not only by parents of the children involved but also by nurses, police, Members of Parliament and, through the medium of the press, the public both in Cleveland and nationally.

3. I was asked to chair the Inquiry, with the following Terms of Reference:

"To examine the arrangements for dealing with suspected cases of child abuse in Cleveland since 1 January 1987, including in particular cases of child sexual abuse, and to make recommendations."

4. I have been assisted in my task by three distinguished Assessors: Professor David Hull, Professor of Child Health at Nottingham University; Mr John Chant, Director of Social Services for Somerset, and Mr Leonard Soper, recently retired as Chief Constable of Gloucestershire.

5. The Inquiry lasted 74 days, starting on August 11th 1987 and ending on the 29th January 1988. We heard evidence in private session for 8 days, all of it given by parents, and thereafter the Inquiry was in public session every day although from time to time part of the day was in private session when we heard evidence which would identify a a particular family.

6. This short extract from the full report is issued with the intention of making widely available a description of what took place in Cleveland in 1987, together with our conclusions and recommendations. There may be members of the public wishing to know what happened and not able to go to the expense of buying the complete version. There may also be professionals who would wish to have our recommendations. However, it is to the complete version that readers must go if they wish to be aware of the full complexities of our Inquiry.

7. In the full Report we set out in detail events as they took place from the perspective of each agency involved, together with detailed comment on the parts played by individuals and agencies. We also comment on the problems of child sexual abuse and deal briefly with arrangements for dealing with physical abuse in Cleveland in 1987. We attempt to portray the perspectives of children and parents in Cleveland. In part 2 of the Report we consider the expert evidence from which some of our recommendations are drawn. In particular we consider aspects of the medical evidence, and the complex issue of 'disclosure'—which we have called 'Listening to the Child'. We also set out some of the issues for social work practice in this field, and look at the Courts and the legal process. In part 4 numerous appendices give additional information, some of which may be useful to professionals. This short version does not attempt to provide more than the story of events, our short conclusions and recommendations.

8. The Assessors and I are unanimous in the conclusions and in the recommendations of the Report, which owe much to their wise advice.

9. Despite all the advice and assistance I have received, the Report remains my sole responsibility.

2. The Story of the Cleveland 'Crisis'

Prior to 1987

1. In Cleveland during 1985 and 1986 a number of people had been expressing concern about the response of the agencies to child sexual abuse, notably a nursing officer responsible for dealing with child abuse in South Tees, Mrs Dunn. A working party of the Area Review Committee under the chairmanship of the National Society for the Prevention of Cruelty to Children representative, Mr Michie, had experienced difficulties in gaining agreement to revised guidelines from all the agencies, particularily from the Police. The efforts of the working party had been protracted but an acceptable draft had been placed in October 1986 before the committee shortly before its demise.

2. In June 1986 Cleveland County Council Social Services Department, as part of their programme to give child protection a greater priority, had appointed Mrs Richardson to the new post of Child Abuse Consultant.

January 1987

3. On the 1st January 1987 Dr Higgs arrived in Cleveland on her appointment as a consultant paediatrician in South Tees Health District. She was based mainly at the Maternity Hospital and at Middlesbrough General Hospital. There she joined, among others, Dr Wyatt and Dr Morrell. She also had sessions at North Tees General Hospital. Dr Higgs was concerned about the services available in Cleveland for deprived and abused children. Before her arrival in Middlesbrough, she had consulted Mrs Richardson on the prevalence of child abuse and the arrangements in Cleveland. She had expressed the hope of working in a community in a deprived area.

4. Soon after her arrival Dr Higgs called on the Director of Social Services, Mr Bishop, and met Mr Walton, his Senior Assistant Director, and Mrs Richardson. She joined in various multi-disciplinary and community projects and became vice-chairman of the newly formed Joint Child Abuse Committee which took over from the Area Review Committee.

5. Mrs Richardson was on the same committee and she was invited to chair a working party to bring up to date guidelines formulated in 1984 by the earlier committee, the Area Review Committee, for the various agencies to work together in the field of child abuse. The purpose of the new working party was to redraft the guidelines and to make more suitable arrangements for dealing with the special requirements of child sexual abuse.

6. Dr Higgs had, in the summer of 1986 in her previous post in Newcastle, examined two Cleveland children in the care of the Cleveland County Council. She suspected sexual abuse and on examination saw for the first time the phenomenon of what has been termed 'reflex relaxation and anal dilatation.' She had recently learnt from Dr Wynne, a consultant paediatrician at Leeds, that this sign is found in children subject to anal abuse. On the basis of various physical findings, including this sign, she diagnosed anal abuse.

February

7. Soon after her arrival in South Tees, her advice was sought about a little girl of 6 with vaginal bleeding. She had been taken by her mother to a doctor who as it happened was also a woman police surgeon. This doctor was concerned and consulted Mrs Richardson who initially recommended a police surgeon, but on learning that the referring doctor was herself a police surgeon, suggested Dr Higgs. Dr Higgs found evidence of vaginal and anal interference and the signs included anal dilatation. The child indicated that her grandfather was responsible. The Police were called and arrested the grandfather, who denied the abuse. He was charged and bailed on the condition that he reside in a bail hostel, and the little girl returned home.

March

8. In March Dr Higgs examined the little girl again and found the signs had reappeared; she diagnosed further abuse and informed Social Services. The grandfather on this occasion could not be the perpetrator, and the little girl said it was her father. Social Services informed the Police. The Police were embarrassed by this revelation and dropped charges against the grandfather. Inspector Whitfield consulted the senior police surgeon, Dr Irvine. The police wanted him to examine the child. Dr Irvine telephoned Dr Higgs. He said she refused to let him examine the child. He expressed the firm view that the sign was unreliable as a basis for diagnosis. On the following day both Dr Higgs and Dr Irvine were at the case conference on the child. Dr Irvine again said he could not accept the grounds for the diagnosis and that Dr Higgs was placing too much reliance upon the observations of Drs Hobbs and Wynne.

9. Dr Irvine went away and consulted Dr Raine Roberts, a well-known police surgeon from Manchester; she supported his stand.

10. The little girl was admitted to hospital and a week later the sign was observed again by Dr Higgs. Dr Higgs saw this child a fourth time in June, when the child was with foster parents, and again the sign was present. Dr Higgs concluded on each occasion that this indicated there had been further sexual abuse.

11. Later in March a little boy of 2 was referred to hospital by his family practitioner as an emergency with constipation. Dr Higgs examined him and noted scars around the anus and the sign of anal dilatation. She considered the possibility of sexual abuse and asked his parents to bring in the elder brother aged 10 and sister aged 9 for examination. They were seen at hospital in the evening and Dr Higgs found signs of anal abuse in the boy and anal and vaginal abuse in the girl. This was the first time that Dr Higgs had diagnosed sexual abuse on the basis of the physical signs alone. She asked Dr Morrell to examine the three children and he agreed with her conclusions. None of the children had made any complaint of abuse. After a request for a second opinion, Dr Higgs directed the children be taken to Leeds to be examined by Dr Wynne. She confirmed the physical findings and endorsed the diagnoses of sexual abuse.

12. Photographs of the children had been taken by a police photographer, and the Police later objected to the use of a police photographer for this purpose. Subsequently photographs of children were taken by a medical photographer.

13. The Police decided to interview the two elder children and did so on Saturday and Sunday; no social worker was present when the children were seen. The elder boy was believed at one time to be the possible perpetrator. According to his father he was 'grilled' by the Police. The boy was upset. This was a matter of some concern to the social workers later involved in the case.

14. Social workers obtained place of safety orders and the children were placed with separate foster parents. The two older children were interviewed on a number of occasions over a period of months, by social workers and a clinical psychologist, Mrs Bacon, who believed the children had been sexually abused and that they were making disclosures of abuse by their father. The children were made wards of court and after the hearing were returned home to their parents. The Judge held that they had not been sexually abused.

15. Dr Wyatt, who had little previous experience in child sexual abuse, was shown the sign by Dr Higgs on one of these three children and found it striking.

16. Some days later a seven year old girl was referred to Dr Higgs by her family practitioner because the child alleged that her father and his girl friend told her to take her clothes off, they played 'doctors' with her and squirted tea up her front. She had had a vaginal discharge for about 5 years. On examination there were abnormal signs relating to the vaginal opening.

April

17. In early April, a 3 year old girl was brought to the Accident and Emergency Department because a school nurse had noticed excessive bruising. She was admitted under the care of Dr Wyatt. He found signs consistent with sexual abuse and asked to see the two elder children. The boy was fine, but the 6 year old girl had anal and vaginal signs, including anal dilatation. This was the first time that Dr Wyatt had observed the sign in one of his patients. All three children went to foster parents and later the elder girl made complaints to her teacher and the foster mother of interference by her step-father.

18. The two children seen by Dr Higgs the previous summer in Newcastle had been placed with experienced foster parents in Cleveland. At the end of April Dr Higgs did a routine check-up preparatory to giving evidence in a pending Juvenile Court hearing. She found anal dilatation and diagnosed anal abuse. The parents had no access to the children for several months and suspicion fell on the foster family. The foster parents were asked to bring their three daughters to be examined in hospital and all were diagnosed as sexually abused.

19. The Director of Social Services, Mr Bishop, was informed that children in the care of the Council had been abused in a foster home and he asked for a second opinion. The 2 foster children and the 3 children of the foster parents were taken to Leeds and examined by Dr Wynne who confirmed the physical signs of sexual abuse in each child.

3

20. A number of children had gone through the foster household, both as foster children and some for whom the foster parents had acted as child minders. Social workers brought 6 more children to be examined by Dr Higgs. Together with the 2 foster children, the 3 children of the foster parents and these 6, 11 children in all were examined of which 10 were found by Dr Higgs to have signs of anal abuse and admitted to the ward.

21. Some of these children were no longer in the foster home or in contact with the foster father. None of the children in this group had made a complaint and no adult had made any allegation of sexual abuse. The children of the foster family became wards and were later returned home by the Judge.

May

22. The weekend after this group of children had been admitted to the ward happened to be the first Bank Holiday weekend in May and there was not the full complement of social workers available. Mrs Richardson helped social workers in the interviews of some of the children.

23. Other children entirely separate from those associated with the foster family were seen during the first week of May in Dr Higgs' outpatient clinic. On the 5th May, 7 of the children were diagnosed as sexually abused. One child, who suffered from a medical condition and was referred for excessive bruising, was a long term patient of Dr Wyatt. Dr Higgs found signs of anal and vaginal abuse and the child's two brothers were seen. A little girl of 1 was referred with rectal bleeding and bowel problems. On examination Dr Higgs found anal dilatation, fissures and a fresh scar. This child was seen by Dr Stanton and Dr Wynne who both confirmed Dr Higgs' findings. Another little girl of 2 was seen on a routine check-up for failure to thrive. She and two other related children were considered by Dr Higgs to have signs of anal abuse. She was already in care. The 3 children remained briefly on the ward and then went to a foster home. They became wards of court and later returned home on conditions by order of the Judge. A girl of 11 was referred by her family practitioner with poor weight gain and eating problems. Dr Higgs found signs of anal and vaginal abuse. Her young half-sister was called and was thought to have signs consistent with sexual abuse. The elder girl later made complaints against her step-father. After a wardship hearing she went to live with her natural father and his new wife. Her half sister went home. In total during the first week of May, 23 children were seen by Dr Higgs and diagnosed as sexually abused and admitted to the Middlesbrough General Hospital.

24. During May there was a steady stream of referrals to Dr Higgs and Dr Wyatt. These included children referred by social workers, health visitors, and a guardian ad litem. The reasons for referral included a mother who was worried that her boy friend might have sexually abused her child, who was found to have a very sore, red perineum, anal dilatation and multiple anal fissures. There were also several children with perineal injuries. In mid-May social workers brought in a family of 5 children for examination because of concern about sexual abuse. A boy aged 7 in the family had made a complaint to his mother and then to a social worker. That family was not admitted to hospital but went with their mother to a group home.

25. A week later social workers referred another family of 3 as a result of the comments of the eldest child of 10 at school and the concern of her headmistress. Dr Higgs examined the first child with the consent of the mother, and found signs she felt were consistent with sexual abuse. Before she could examine the second child, the father arrived on the ward and removed the 3 children. He took them to a secret address. He was at that time required to report daily to the police who were unable to persuade him to divulge the whereabouts of the children. However he agreed to the examination of the children by a police surgeon, and Dr Beeby was taken to the secret address. He examined the children in an upstairs room and found no abnormality. They were then returned home by their father; removed on a place of safety order obtained by Social Services and taken back to hospital. This time Dr Higgs examined all 3 children and diagnosed sexual abuse in respect of all 3. The following day Dr Irvine examined the 3 children and agreed with the conclusions of Dr Beeby. Two weeks later, Dr McCowen, paediatrician from Northallerton, considered the signs suspicious and later in June Dr Roberts and Dr Paul examined the children and considered there was no abnormality. These children were first dealt with, at a very prolonged hearing, on an interim care application before the Teesside Juvenile Court and thereafter in wardship. The children were returned home but remain wards. The Social Services Department were extremely concerned at the removal of the children from the hospital ward by the father and the difficulties of tracing their whereabouts.

26. Also during May there were referrals to Dr Higgs other than by Social Services; for example, a Senior House Officer while examining a child of 2 with a febrile fit noted an abnormal anus. Dr Higgs found signs of anal and vaginal abuse in this child and her 2 sisters. The father was charged with several

sexual offences and committed suicide while awaiting trial. A Senior Clinical Medical Officer, as a result of concern in the neighbourhood about the possibility of sexual abuse, referred a family of 7 children, 4 of the children showed signs of sexual abuse and all 7 were admitted to the hospital. A nurse noticed an abnormal anus in a 2 year old boy admitted with asthma and Dr Higgs concluded that there were signs consistent with sexual abuse. He was examined by Dr Steiner who did not agree with Dr Higgs and the child returned home.

27. Over the second Bank Holiday weekend in May there was a new wave of admissions to Middlesbrough General Hospital. The numbers were augmented by the admission of the 7 children from one family and 3 children from another family. Altogether in May, 52 children from 17 families were examined for sexual abuse and 41 of them were considered to have physical signs of sexual abuse.

28. Most of the children had no medical problem requiring nursing or medical attention and their presence on the ward caused difficulties for the nurses. Social Services managed to place most of the children out of hospital with foster parents or in residential care, but their field workers were very stretched. Mrs de Lacy Dunne, the adoption and fostering officer, took control of all foster placements. By June she and her resources became overwhelmed and ran out of space for the children.

29. In May the hospital had the resources to cope, but it was an unprecedented number of children with an unfamiliar problem and alarm bells began to ring. Dr Drury, the Hospital Unit Manager, had been informed of the numbers admitted in the first week of May. He got in touch with the Social Services Department to express his concern both at the numbers and the problems in the hospital, particularily for the nurses. Dr Drury met Dr Higgs and they discussed among other matters the disagreement between herself and Dr Irvine.

30. At a meeting in mid-May of the South Tees Community Health Council, Mr Urch, its Secretary, told Mr Bishop about mounting public anxiety over the admissions to hospital and the diagnosis of child sexual abuse.

31. Mrs Richardson, who had earlier predicted an increase in detection of sexual abuse, was alarmed by the numbers and the lack of resources to deal with them. On the 12th May she wrote a memorandum to Mr Bishop referring to a 'crisis', the likelihood that the numbers would increase and the need for more resources.

32. At the invitation of Mr Bishop she attended a meeting of the Social Services Directorate in mid-May. They discussed the alarming increase in referrals for child sexual abuse, but the differences between Dr Higgs and Dr Irvine and the controversy over the anal dilatation test and the diagnosis of sexual abuse were not referred to. Mrs Richardson did not recognise the importance of the dispute and did not inform the Director.

The Police in April and May

33. By the end of April and the beginning of May the Police were having doubts about the diagnosis of sexual abuse based upon the anal dilatation test. These doubts were reinforced by the strong views of Dr Irvine. At a meeting chaired by a Chief Superintendent on the 8th May, Dr Irvine was asked his views and made plain to senior police officers that he regarded the anal dilatation test as unreliable.

34. Also at the end of April, as a result of Dr Higgs requesting police photographers to photograph the ano-genital region of the 3 children in March, and on the instructions of Detective Superintendent White, Inspector Walls, the head of the Scientific Aids Department went to see Dr Higgs and explain the concern his Department had at taking these photographs. His photographers were embarrassed and felt the children were upset. The meeting was more in the nature of a confrontation, with Inspector Walls telling Dr Higgs what he thought. It did not improve relations between the Police and Dr Higgs.

35. Detective Superintendent White went twice in May to Middlesbrough General Hospital to discuss both the problem over the photographs and the difficulties caused by the diagnosis of child sexual abuse.

36. In the absence of prompt medical statements and with these doubts the Police investigated but without much confidence in the outcome. There was also a feeling, expressed by Inspector Makepeace of the Community Relations Department, that the good relations which he believed existed between police officers and social workers on the ground had deteriorated since the appointment of Mrs Richardson in her new role. These feelings among the Police gathered momentum.

Joint Child Abuse Committee Working Party—Meeting in May and its Consequences

37. The working party of the Joint Child Abuse Committee, chaired by Mrs Richardson (see paragraph 5), included a representative of the Police, Chief Inspector Taylor; a nursing officer, Mrs Dunn; Mr Michie from the NSPCC; an educational social worker, Mr Town; and a probation officer. Between February and May they met on several occasions and agreed most of the outstanding issues which had troubled their predecessors on the Area Review Committee. The two main issues which remained were:

1. the degree of co-operation between the police and social workers in the investigation of sexual abuse;

2. who should perform the medical examination and whether the police surgeon should be consulted.

It was agreed that Mrs Richardson and Chief Inspector Taylor should arrange a meeting with Dr Higgs and Dr Irvine to try and come to an agreement on the issue which could be placed before the next meeting of the working party on the 1st June. The meeting was arranged for the 28th May.

38. At that meeting in addition to Mrs Richardson and Dr Higgs there were Dr Irvine, Detective Superintendent White, Inspector Makepeace, and Chief Inspector Taylor. The previous day Dr Irvine had for the first time examined children found by Dr Higgs to have been sexually abused. His negative findings confirmed Dr Irvine in his view as to the unreliability of the anal dilatation test. Dr Higgs had by then diagnosed as anally abused a considerable number of children, some confirmed by other paediatricians, and was convinced of the reliability of the test. When the meeting began to discuss the medical aspects of sexual abuse, Mrs Richardson put forward some new proposals, the effect of which was to provide for examination in all cases by the paediatrician. When challenged on this it became clear that Mrs Richardson did not see any future for police surgeons in the examination of children said to be sexually abused. Dr Irvine then said that Dr Higgs was incompetent and misguided and that her 'mentors' in Leeds, Drs Wynne and Hobbs, were equally misguided. Dr Higgs was firm in her viewpoint. Inspector Makepeace supported Dr Irvine and Mrs Richardson supported Dr Higgs. The meeting became heated and all those present found it disagreeable.

39. Detective Superintendent White expressed the Police conclusion that the Police would treat the diagnosis of Dr Higgs with a degree of caution. Each group left the meeting with their preconceived ideas reinforced, and this led to a major breakdown in the relationship between the Police and the social workers.

40. After the meeting Mrs Richardson and Mr Hughes together drafted a memorandum for Mr Bishop. It was largely the work of Mrs Richardson. Mr Bishop was given this memorandum and signed it on the 29th May. Its main effects were to provide for routine applications for place of safety orders in cases of suspected sexual abuse, to suspend access to the parents and to exclude the police surgeon from making a second examination.

41. Detective Superintendent White on the 29th May sent out a Force circular in which he instructed the Police to view Dr Higgs' diagnosis on sexual abuse with caution, and to look for substantial corroboration of her findings before taking positive action. Although Superintendent White had told Mrs Richardson of the police response, neither agency officially informed the other of the steps they were taking.

42. The meeting of the working party of the Joint Child Abuse Committee was scheduled to take place on the 1st June. The Assistant Chief Constable Mr Smith instructed Chief Inspector Taylor not to attend. The working party went on in his absence and with no disagreement the proposals put forward on the 28th May were accepted by the working party as their recommendations to the Joint Child Abuse Committee on the medical issue. They included: that the hospital was the most appropriate setting for the examination of a child by a paediatrician, and where a consultant paediatrician is able to give a statement to the Police it is not necessary for a police surgeon to re-examine the child.

June

43. In June children continued to be referred in ever growing numbers, mainly by Social Services. They included; children who had constipation, failure to thrive, an itchy bottom, urinary tract infection, bruised perineum, soiling etc. A nurse saw a gaping anus in a child admitted to hospital with tonsilitis and brought it to Dr Higgs' attention. There was a family of 7 children who had behavioural problems and poor growth, and several members of this family were diagnosed as showing signs of sexual abuse.

44. Dr Wyatt was asked by Social Services to see 2 boys from a special school who had been found with others indulging in inappropriate sexual behaviour. Dr Wyatt found signs of anal interference in both boys and offered to examine all the children in the special school. In the event the situation was dealt with by the Education Department. 6 of the children from 2 of the families concerned were admitted to the ward. One boy of 11 had considerable behavioural problems and had been under the care of a child psychiatrist for several years. In further 4 families the index (first) child examined during June had behavioural problems and had previously been seen by a child psychiatrist. Also about this time Dr Higgs saw a 3 year old girl with a vaginal discharge caused by gonorrhoea. The infection was present in her rectum. Her 2 year old brother also had a sexually transmitted infection. The girl had vaginal signs, both had signs of anal abuse. The children's uncle and a friend were convicted of sexual offences. Another little girl had anal warts. She had been referred by her family practitioner on suspicion of sexual abuse. The Independent Panel which examined this child came to the conclusion that the child should return home. The anal warts were not shown to be sexually transmitted.

45. During June children in two more foster homes were considered to have been sexually abused. In one case it was a handicapped child living with adoptive parents who was diagnosed as abused. Before informing the agencies Dr Higgs arranged for Dr Wynne to give a second opinion on the child and she confirmed the diagnosis. This child and his sister became wards and were returned home by the Judge on the basis that no sexual abuse had occurred.

46. Also during June, members of the Emergency Duty Team of social workers were asked to obtain place of safety orders late at night mainly by Dr Wyatt. In one case there had been an agreement with the parents that the children would remain on the ward; in another the children had been allowed to go home and had gone to bed, and then had to be brought back to hospital. On one evening Dr Wyatt asked for 11 place of safety orders, 7 relating to a family already well-known to the Social Services.

47. On the evening of the 12th June Dr Wyatt was making a late evening round, a usual occurrence with him. Dr Higgs was on call and she went round the ward with him. The ward contained 12 children of 8 families where sexual abuse had been diagnosed. During that day between them they had identified 4 index children as sexually abused. Later that evening nurses told them of abnormal anal findings in 2 further children. They examined the children and diagnosed sexual abuse. Those 2 children had between them 8 siblings. They examined 4 children that night because of the possibility of sexual abuse. They were dissuaded from examining a 5th child because the nurse said that the mother and child were asleep. Some nurses became upset about these examinations and two nurses made a written complaint.

48. The following day it was necessary to transfer 6 children to North Tees General Hospital because the wards in Middlesbrough General Hospital could not cope with the siblings of the children identified the night before.

49. The events of the 12th June and the consequential intake of the siblings created the third large wave of admissions.

50. On the 18th June there was a considerable number of parents at the hospital and there was a confrontation between Dr Wyatt and an angry father. The police were called and helped to calm the situation. The deputy administrator at the hospital took the parents to another building and helped them to set out their complaints for transmission to the hospital authorities.

51. The following day Mr Stuart Bell MP was told of the situation at the hospital and paid it several visits during the following week. He heard the parents' complaints. Some parents had just begun to form themselves into a parents' support group with the assistance of the Rev. Michael Wright.

52. During June there were meetings between professionals and the different disciplines to try to resolve the problems which arose.

— On the **1st June** Mr Bishop together with Mrs Richardson met Mr Donaldson, Dr Drury, Dr Ramiah, the new community physician, and Dr Higgs. Mr Bishop questioned Dr Higgs very closely on her diagnostic techniques and was satisfied that she was confident of what she was doing. None of the other doctors present queried her method of diagnosis.

— On the **5th June** the Chief Constable and the Assistant Chief Constable Mr Smith met Mr Bishop and Mr Walton, his senior Assistant Director and they discussed the situation. Neither of the Chief Officers was entirely in the picture and the only suggestion made was for the deputies to meet the

Crown Prosecution Service. This they did with no result. The Chief Constable and the Director made no arrangement to meet again and did not do so.

— Shortly after that Dr Higgs and Dr Wyatt called on Mr Bishop and refused to see anybody else. They praised him for his stand over child sexual abuse and said that the detection of abuse was a breakthrough in the care of children and could explain many problems of child health which had previously not responded to treatment. Mr Bishop took the opportunity to tell them about the strain on the resources of the Department and asked them if they could proceed more slowly to allow Social Services to obtain more resources. They told him it was not professionally acceptable to them and that other agencies needed to recognise that this was a major development in child health.

— On the **11th June** Mr Cooke, the Clerk to the Justices went to see Mr Bishop. Many place of safety orders were expiring and applications were being made for interim care orders on the children. Two days before in the Teesside Juvenile Court there had been the unprecedented number of 45 applications for interim care orders. Mr Cooke asked Mr Bishop if he could arrange for 28 day applications for place of safety orders to be made to the magistrate. The difficulties of dealing with the large number of cases were compounded by the unusual opposition to the granting of the interim order. These applications were being contested and disputed medical evidence was having to be considered by the magistrates at an early stage in the proceedings. Mr Cooke noticed that this might have been due to the refusal or restriction of access to the parents which was also most unusual. A few days later Mr Cooke returned to see Mr Bishop, on this occasion accompanied by the Chairman of the Juvenile Panel, expressing the concerns of the Juvenile Bench about the numbers of cases which were threatening to overwhelm the Courts; the great concern of the magistrates at the refusal of access to parents; and the most unusual situation of disputed medical evidence. Again Mr Cooke suggested application for longer place of safety orders to relieve pressure on the courts. Later in June some disputed care applications were restarted in the High Court as wardship applications.

— On the **15th June** Mr Bishop consulted the Social Services Inspectorate as to whether second opinions might be obtained and was advised to go to the District Health Authority. He immediately got in touch with Mr Donaldson and asked him to arrange second opinions on the diagnoses of the two doctors.

— On the **16th June** Mr Donaldson consulted Dr Donaldson, the Regional Medical Officer of the Northern Regional Health Authority concerning the complaints of the two nurses about the evening of the 12th June and asked for advice and help. This was the first that Northern Region had heard of the crisis and they then became involved. Northern Region decided to deal with all the complaints about the two doctors. The following day Dr Donaldson and Mr Donaldson met and Mr Donaldson asked for help to deal with the request from Mr Bishop for second medical opinions.

— Also on the **16th June** there was a meeting of the Joint Child Abuse Consultative Committee at which senior representatives of Social Services and the Police attended. They did not tell the elected members about the difficulties being experienced between the two agencies. At the same time there were meetings between the Chief Executive and leading members of the County Council where the seriousness of the situation was fully explored.

— On the **18th June** after the incident with the parent on the ward, Mr Donaldson discussed the situation with both paediatricians and asked them to hold back. They refused and said that if they saw child sexual abuse they had a duty to act.

— Mr Donaldson then asked three senior consultants to interview the two doctors and find out if they were acting within the bounds of medical practice. At the meeting on the 23rd June the two paediatricians assured the three consultants that they were acting correctly.

53. The Chairman of Northern Region, Professor Sir Bernard Tomlinson, became involved and he and Dr Donaldson invited the two paediatricians to the headquarters of the Regional Health Authority in Newcastle to find out if they were acting correctly. They had a four hour meeting. Drs Higgs and Wyatt were given the complaints and asked to comment on them, which they said they would do after they had consulted their legal advisers. After the meeting at which the two doctors were cross-examined at length by the two Regional Officers, both Professor Sir Bernard Tomlinson and Dr Donaldson could find no reason to recommend their suspension from duties to the Regional Committee. There were thereafter various meetings which included legal advisers to consider the complaints and the position of the doctors.

54. The Northern Regional Health Authority took over the arrangements for second opinions requested by Social Services and with the help of Professor Kolvin, Consultant Child Psychiatrist at Newcastle, set up a panel of paediatricians and child psychiatrists to see jointly the children who had been diagnosed as

sexually abused. They started to see children at the end of June. Thereafter Northern Region set up a second panel called the Regional Reference Group, made up of paediatricians within the area of Northern Region to see any children who were subsequently diagnosed as sexually abused in South Tees District Area.

55. By the end of June parents had arranged their own second opinions and a number of doctors, principally Dr Roberts from Manchester, Dr Paul from London and Dr Clarke from Liverpool, saw many of the children concerned.

56. On **Friday 26th June** Dr Irvine was interviewed on television in the early evening and said that Dr Higgs was wrong in her diagnosis of sexual abuse in respect of a particular family.

57. Later that evening on the television programme Nightline, Mr Bishop and Mr Bell MP were among those who were present. Dr Irvine's interview was shown. Mr Bishop said he had no alternative but to act on the diagnosis of the paediatrician.

58. On the **29th June**, Mr Bell put down a Private Notice Question in the House Of Commons asking the Minister if he would make a statement on the recent increase in the number of cases of alleged child abuse in Cleveland.

59. At the request of the Minister of State for Health reports were provided very quickly by the Social Services Inspectorate, the Northern Regional Health Authority. The Police provided a report for the Home Office.

60. At the end of June, with the help of Middlesbrough General Hospital, Social Services set up the Child Resource Centre in the grounds of the hospital and children and their parents were able to spend the day there and be interviewed there.

July

61. On the **1st July** the Joint Child Abuse Committee met to consider the recommendations of the working party. Mr Walton, with the help of Mr Smith, took charge of the draft guidelines and in a few days secured agreement to a revised draft which was almost immediately put into effect both by the Social Services and the Police. The agreed guidelines included that the hospital is often the most appropriate setting for medical examination; that the child should be referred as soon as possible to a consultant paediatrician; that the roles of the police surgeon and paediatrician are complementary; early consultation is essential; there should be joint examination where possible.

62. Also on the **1st July** the Police set up the Child Abuse Unit at Yarm, to co-ordinate the investigation of child sexual abuse in the County.

63. On the **7th July** Mr Bell gave the Minister a 'dossier' of cases he had investigated. On the **9th July** the Minister announced in a statement to the House of Commons the setting up of a Statutory Inquiry.

64. This is a brief description of the events in Cleveland which led to the crisis.

3. Final Conclusions

1. We have learned during the Inquiry that sexual abuse occurs in children of all ages, including the very young, to boys as well as girls, in all classes of society and frequently within the privacy of the family. The sexual abuse can be very serious and on occasions includes vaginal, anal and oral intercourse. The problems of child sexual abuse have been recognised to an increasing extent over the past few years by professionals in different disciplines. This presents new and particularly difficult problems for the agencies concerned in child protection. In Cleveland an honest attempt was made to address these problems by the agencies. In Spring 1987 it went wrong.

2. The reasons for the crisis are complex. In essence they included:

— lack of a proper understanding by the main agencies of each others' functions in relation to child sexual abuse;

— a lack of communication between the agencies;

— differences of views at middle management level which were not recognised by senior staff. These eventually affected those working on the ground.

3. These tensions came out into the open with Dr Higgs' appointment as a consultant paediatrician to the Middlesbrough General Hospital. She was known to have an interest in the problems of child abuse. As a result of her understanding of the work of Dr Hobbs and Dr Wynne in Leeds, she formed the view that physical signs could help to identify sexual abuse and assist those seeking to protect abused children. She referred the first few children in whom she made the diagnosis to Dr Wynne for a second opinion. In each she received confirmation of her diagnosis, and as a consequence she proceeded with increasing confidence. The presence of the physical signs was elevated from grounds of 'strong suspicion' to an unequivocal 'diagnosis' of sexual abuse.

4. Dr Wyatt, another consultant paediatrician at Middlesbrough General Hospital, became equally convinced of the significance of the physical signs and he enthusiastically supported her.

5. Dr Higgs and Dr Wyatt became the centre point of recognition of the problem. Between them in 5 months they diagnosed 121 children as being sexually abused—78 by Dr Higgs, 43 by Dr Wyatt. Children were referred to them in various ways; some were brought by social workers because of a suspicion of sexual abuse or allegations or complaints; others were referred by family practitioners, health visitors, or community medical officers because of a suspicion of sexual abuse; a few from within the hospital were referred by junior medical staff or by nurses. In some the diagnosis arose on children attending outpatient clinics with medical conditions in which the possibility of sexual abuse had not been previously raised. Many were siblings of or connected with these children.

6. By reaching a firm conclusion on the basis of physical signs and acting as they would for non-accidental injury or physical abuse; by separating children from their parents and by admitting most of the children to hospital, they compromised the work of the social workers and the Police. The medical diagnosis assumed a central and determining role in the management of the child and the family.

7. It was entirely proper for the two paediatricians to play their part in the identification of sexual abuse in children referred to them. They were responsible for the care of their patients. Nonetheless they had a responsibility to examine their own actions; to consider whether their practice was always correct and whether it was in the best interests of the children their patients. They are to be criticised for not doing so and for the certainty and over-confidence with which they pursued the detection of sexual abuse in children referred to them. They were not solely nor indeed principally responsible for the subsequent management of the children concerned. However, the certainty of their findings in relation to children diagnosed by them without prior complaint, posed particular problems for the Police and Social Services.

8. The response of the Social Services Department to the diagnoses of the two doctors was determined in the main by the newly appointed Child Abuse Consultant, Mrs Richardson, who supported and agreed with Dr Higgs' approach. She advised that immediately the diagnosis was made the child should be moved to a 'place of safety' for further investigation and evaluation and this was ensured by obtaining a place of safety order from a Magistrate. This practice was confirmed by the issuing of a memorandum by the Director of Social Services which in practice had the effect of endorsing the medical diagnoses of the two paediatricians. In most cases the social workers' own professional responsibilities required them to make a wider assessment before taking action. The number of children separated from their parents increased

dramatically and required both the consultants and Social Services managers to reappraise their practice. This they failed to do. They had a responsibility to look into the numbers of referrals and the method of diagnosis. As the crisis developed, both doctors and social workers had a duty to consider their priorities, particularly with children from families with long-standing problems who were well known to Social Services.

9. Another element was the attitude of the Police encouraged by their senior police surgeon, Dr Irvine, who took the view that Dr Higgs was mistaken in her diagnoses. The Police retreated from the multi-disciplinary approach into an entrenched position. They can be criticised for allowing a rift to develop and taking no effective step to break the deadlock. There was no reaction at senior level to the problems being raised and passed on to them by operational officers. The Police blamed the attitude and approach of Mrs Richardson for their reactions. They should not have allowed personalities to stand in the way of an objective assessment of the situation and the need to resolve it. Their requirement that the diagnoses of Dr Higgs should be reviewed by the senior police surgeon was unhelpful in the circumstances.

10. There was a failure by middle and senior managers in each agency to take action appropriate to the seriousness of the situation. The disagreements between the Police and Social Services were allowed to drift and the crisis to develop. In particular, the Chief Constable and the Director of Social Services failed to understand the depth of the disagreement between their staff and as a consequence failed to take some joint action to bring their two agencies together.

11. The lack of appropriate legal advice at case conferences contributed to the failure of those most closely involved with the children to appreciate that the medical opinions they had acted upon might not provide a satisfactory basis for applications in care proceedings. This deprived them of a useful check in consideration of the advisability of the removal of the children from home.

12. There was an understandable response from parents when the diagnosis of sexual abuse was made. Their child was admitted to hospital; a place of safety order was served on them; access was restricted for the purpose of 'disclosure work'. They were uncertain of their responsibilities, distressed and angry. They did not know what to do or where to turn. They were isolated. As the numbers grew many of them formed themselves into a support group and they then received increasing support from others both locally and nationally. The media reported the situation and the crisis became public knowledge.

13. Most of the 121 children diagnosed by Drs Higgs and Wyatt as sexually abused were separated from their parents and their home, 70% or so by place of safety orders. 67 of the children became wards of court. In the wardship cases 27 were dewarded and went home with the proceedings dismissed; 24 went home to both parents, there were conditions which included supervision orders and conditions as to medical examination of the children, and 2 of them went home on interim care orders. Of those children not made wards of court, a further 26 were the subject of place of safety orders. Of these, 17 are at home, 6 still with a social worker allocated. In all 21 children remain in care. We understand that out of the 121 children, 98 are now at home.

14. It is unacceptable that the disagreements and failure of communication of adults should be allowed to obscure the needs of children both long term and short term in so sensitive, difficult and important a field. The children had unhappy experiences which should not be allowed to happen again.

15. It is however important to bear in mind that those who have a responsibility to protect children at risk, such as social workers, health visitors, police and doctors have in the past been criticised for failure to act in sufficient time and to take adequate steps to protect children who are being damaged. In Cleveland the general criticism by the public has been of over-enthusiasm and zeal in the actions taken. It is difficult for professionals to balance the conflicting interests and needs in the enormously important and delicate field of child sexual abuse. We hope that professionals will not as a result of the Cleveland experience stand back and hesitate to act to protect the children.

16. In many Inquiries it is social workers who are under scrutiny for their failure to act in time. We are concerned that in advising a calm, measured and considered approach to the problem of child sexual abuse, we are not seen to imply either that there are never occasions when immediate action may need to be taken or that there is not a problem to be faced and children to be protected. It is a delicate and difficult line to tread between taking action too soon and not taking it soon enough. Social Services whilst putting the needs of the child first must respect the rights of the parents; they also must work if possible with the parents for the benefit of the children. These parents themselves are often in need of help. Inevitably a degree of conflict develops between those objectives.

17. We are also concerned about the extent of the misplaced adverse criticism social workers have received from the media and elswhere. There is a danger that social workers, including those in Cleveland,

will be demoralised. Some may hesitate to do what is right. Social workers need the support of the public to continue in the job the public needs them to do. It is time the public and the press gave it to them.

18. Whilst it was important to try and identify what went wrong, it is equally important not to let that identification impede progress in the future, in Cleveland and elsewhere. We make criticisms of individuals. Those criticisms must not be permitted to obscure the wider failings of agencies; nor would we wish to suggest that the identification and management of sexual abuse within the family is easy. It obviously is not.

19. We hope that the troubles of 1987 will recede for those concerned with the protection of children in Cleveland, and that they will work together, to tackle the exacting task of helping children who are subject to sexual abuse to the lasting benefit of the children, the families and their community.

How society acknowledges the existence of, recognises and then handles child sexual abuse poses difficult and complex problems. There are some issues of importance upon which we did not receive evidence and which we have not addressed. These include specifically the nature of abusers and the reasons for sexual abuse of children; the effectiveness and appropriateness of the strategies used once the problem has been identified; and the response of society and the agencies to those who abuse.

There are also some issues upon which we do not make recommendations but which in our view justify further consideration and we set out these with our observations at page 21.

We make the following recommendations:

Recommendations

1. Recognition of sexual abuse

There is a need:

    a. To recognise and describe the extent of the problem of child sexual abuse;

    b. To receive more accurate data of the abuse which is identified.

2. Children

There is a danger that in looking to the welfare of the children believed to be the victims of sexual abuse the children themselves may be overlooked. The child is a person and not an object of concern.

We recommend that:

    a. Professionals recognise the need for adults to explain to children what is going on. Children are entitled to a proper explanation appropriate to their age, to be told why they are being taken away from home and given some idea of what is going to happen to them.

    b. Professionals should not make promises which cannot be kept to a child, and in the light of possible court proceedings should not promise a child that what is said in confidence can be kept in confidence.

    c. Professionals should always listen carefully to what the child has to say and take seriously what is said.

    d. Throughout the proceedings the views and the wishes of the child, particularly as to what should happen to him/her, should be taken into consideration by the professionals involved with their problems.

    e. The views and the wishes of the child should be placed before whichever court deals with the case. We do not however, suggest that those wishes should predominate.

    f. Children should not be subjected to repeated medical examinations solely for evidential purposes. Where appropriate, according to age and understanding, the consent of the child should be obtained before any medical examination or photography.

    g. Children should not be subjected to repeated interviews nor to the probing and confrontational type of 'disclosure' interview for the same purpose, for it in itself can be damaging and harmful to them. The consent of the child should where possible be obtained before the interviews are recorded on video.

    h. The child should be medically examined and interviewed in a suitable and sensitive environment, where there are suitably trained staff available.

i. When a child is moved from home or between hospital and foster home it is important that those responsible for the day to day care of the child not only understand the child's legal status but also have sufficient information to look after the child properly.

j. Those involved in investigation of child sexual abuse should make a conscious effort to ensure that they act throughout in the best interests of the child.

3. Parents

We recommend:

a. The parents should be given the same courtesy as the family of any other referred child. This applies to all aspects of the investigation into the suspicion of child sexual abuse, and should be recognised by all professionals concerned with the family.

b. Parents should be informed and where appropriate consulted at each stage of the investigation by the professional dealing with the child, whether medical, police or social worker. Parents are entitled to know what is going on, and to be helped to understand the steps that are being taken.

c. We discuss below the position of parents in case conferences.

d. Social Services should confirm all important decisions to parents in writing. Parents may not understand the implications of decisions made and they should have the opportunity to give the written decision to their lawyers.

e. Parents should always be advised of their rights of appeal or complaint in relation to any decisions made about them or their children.

f. Social Services should always seek to provide support to the family during the investigation. Parents should not be left isolated and bewildered at this difficult time.

g. The service of the place of safety order on parents should include a written explanation of the meaning of the order, the position of the parents, their continuing responsibilities and rights and advice to seek legal advice.

4. Social Services

We make the following recommendations with regard to Social Services:

Place of Safety Orders

a. Place of safety orders should only be sought for the minimum time necessary to ensure protection of the child.

b. Records related to the use of statutory powers on an emergency basis should be kept and monitored regularly by Social Services Departments.

c. A code of practice for the administration by social workers of emergency orders for the purposes of child protection including the provision of information to parents defining their rights in clear simple language should be drawn up (see also recommendations on the courts).

Access

d. Whenever and however children are received into care social workers should agree with parents the arrangements for access unless there are exceptional reasons related to the childs interests not to do so. In either event the parent should be notified in writing as soon as possible of the access arrangements and the avenues of complaint or appeal open to them if they are aggrieved.

Case Conferences

e. Parents should be informed of case conferences and invited to attend for all or part of the conference unless, in the view of the Chairman of the conference, their presence will preclude a full and proper consideration of the child's interests.

f. Irrespective of whether parents attend the conferences social workers have a primary responsibility to ensure that the case conference has information relating to the family background and the parents' views on the issues under consideration.

g. In complex cases the Chairman of the conference must be able to call upon the attendance of a qualified lawyer to assist in the evaluation of evidence indicative of care proceedings.

h. When a case conference is presented with medical opinions that are in conflict the doctors involved should be asked to review their findings jointly with the interests of the child in mind. If they are unable to establish common ground then they should be asked to identify the basis of their differences. It would then be for the case conference to consider their views in the context of the other information available.

Management

i. Senior managers in Social Services Departments need to ensure that they have efficient systems available to allow accurate monitoring of service activity which will alert them to problems that need to be resolved.

j. Staff engaged in social work practice in the field of child abuse and child sexual abuse need structured arrangements for their professional supervision and personal support. The work is stressful and it is important that their personal needs are not overlooked.

k. We recommend that careful consideration be given to the provision of structured systems of support and supervision for staff undertaking work on Emergency Duty Teams. Operationally such teams should report to a senior line manager.

l. Social Services Departments should maintain an open continuing relationship with the Police to review areas of mutual concern.

5. Police

We make the following recommendations with regard to Police Forces:

a. The Police should examine their organisation to ensure there is an adequate communication network to achieve the recognition and identification of problems at operational level and a system to develop remedies.

b. The Police should develop, monitor and maintain communication and consultation with the other agencies concerned with child protection.

c. The Police should develop and practise inter-agency working, including joint planning and interviews of children in investigation of sexual abuse within the family or caring agency.

d. The Police should recognise and develop their responsibility for the protection of the child as extending beyond the collection of evidence for court proceedings. This should include their attendance at case conferences and assistance to the other child protection agencies.

6. The Medical Profession

We make the following recommendations with regard to the medical profession:

a. They should agree a consistent vocabulary to describe physical signs which may be associated with child sexual abuse.

b. There should be investigation of the natural history and the significance of signs and symptoms which may be associated with child sexual abuse.

c. Consideration be given to inquiring into the significance of the phenomenon of anal dilatation.

d. Doctors engaged in the care of a child in whom the suspicion of sexual abuse is raised must of course give the child the appropriate medical care, but should also recognise the importance of the forensic element.

The doctor concerned should recognise the importance:

i. of taking a full medical history and making a thorough medical examination

ii. of making where appropriate investigations for forensic purposes, for sexually transmitted diseases and for pregnancy in older girls.

iii. of completing full and accurate medical records which should provide the information for the protective agencies and on occasions the courts. [see appendix F] Those records should be made at the time of examination.

iv. of preparing statements for police purposes and/or for Social Services or NSPCC.

We understand that the Standing Medical Advisory Committee to the DHSS are in the course of providing guidelines for the medical profession on this subject.

e. On a medical examination for forensic or other evidential purposes unconnected with the immediate care and treatment of the child the informed consent of the parents should be sought. This may present difficulties for the police surgeon or doctor from the approved panel on the Specialist

Assessment Team [see below] in cases of suspected sexual abuse within the family. This problem needs to be considered further.

f. Medical practitioners who have examined a child for suspected sexual abuse and disagree in their findings and conclusions should discuss their reports and resolve their differences where possible; in the absence of agreement identify the areas of dispute, recognising their purpose is to act in the best interests of the child.

7. Area Review Committees/Joint Child Abuse Committees

We make the following recommendations in respect of the Area Review Committees/ Joint Child Abuse Committees:

a. They should review the arrangements for identifying and monitoring suitable training for professionals working with child sexual abuse;

b. The membership of these committees should include those who have the authority and responsibility to bind their agency to implementing the recommendations of the Committee, and to play a useful part in the decision-making process which accurately reflects the view of the agency they represent.

8. Inter-Agency Co-operation

We strongly recommend:

a. The development of inter-agency co-operation which acknowledges:

i. no single agency—Health, Social Services, Police or voluntary organisation has the pre-eminent responsibility in the assessment of child abuse generally and child sexual abuse specifically. Each agency has a prime responsibility for a particular aspect of the problem. Neither childrens' nor parents' needs and rights can be adequately met or protected unless agencies agree a framework for their inter-action. The statutory duties of Social Service Departments must be recognised;

ii. careful consideration must be given to the detail of working arrangements between doctors, nurses, social workers, police, teachers, staff of voluntary organisations and others responsible for the care of children;

iii. arrangements for collaboration between services must not inhibit prompt action by any professional or agency where this is demanded by the best interests of the child. Agreements over collaborative work should not inhibit or preclude doctors, social workers or policemen from carrying out their primary professional responsibilities. The responsibility for the decisions will remain theirs;

iv. practical issues need to be recognised and resolved at local level in careful discussion between the respective agencies. For example:

— what the level of suspicion of physical or sexual abuse should be before the Police are informed that an offence appears to have been committed;

— when and what parents are told when doctors see signs that may be indicative of sexual abuse;

— in what circumstances social workers should delay seeing parents until they have been interviewed by the Police.

v. managers should accept responsibility for ensuring that agreements reached are implemented in practice. Each agency should give an undertaking not to make unilateral changes in practice or policy without giving prior notice to the others;

vi. the existence of bodies charged with the responsibility to co-ordinate practice between agencies does not relieve Chief Officers such as the Director of Social Services, the Chief Constable, the Director of Education and the Health Service District General Manager of their responsibility to ensure effective co-operation and collaboration between their services or to identify problems and seek solutions.

b. The establishment of Specialist Assessment Teams.

i. The function of the Specialist Assessment Team (SAT) is to undertake a full multi-disciplinary assessment of the child and the family in cases of particular difficulty. Each member of the team will have direct access to information available within their agency. The completion of a medical examination, a social work assessment, and appropriate inquiries by the Police, carried out in a planned and co-ordinated way should allow the Specialist Assessment Team to present their joint assessment and conclusions to the referring agency or a case conference. Whilst each member of the team has a duty to act with care and undertake the full range of responsibilities normally ascribed to the individual's role—including where necessary the continuing investigations—their first and primary responsibility as a team is to make an assessment. The duty to provide on-going treatment or plan for the future should remain with others.

ii. The team should consist of an approved medical practitioner, a senior social worker, and a police officer with sufficient authority to co-ordinate the investigation of cases.

iii. In each area a list of approved doctors should be drawn up. The process of approval might be adapted from the regulations under the Mental Health Act which provide for the approval of doctors for the purpose of that Act. The doctors on the list should have knowledge and experience of the needs of children and an understanding of child abuse in general and child sexual abuse in particular. They should be prepared, at the request of their medical colleagues, Social Services or the Police, to examine a child and participate in a formal multi-disciplinary assessment of the child's presenting concern. This may include collecting forensic evidence; compiling medical evidence for care proceedings; and involve attendance at case conferences and at Court. The doctors included on such a list might be community or hospital paediatricians, or those who have appropriate experience such as women police doctors, police surgeons etc.

iv. The Social Services will need to appoint to an approved list those social workers who are trained, experienced and competent in work in the field of child abuse and child sexual abuse.

v. The Police will need to appoint to an approved list, police officers trained, experienced and competent in the field of child sexual abuse to undertake the work required.

vi. It is probably not in the interests of either the children, families or professionals or the agency for staff-doctors, social workers, or police to specialise solely in child sexual abuse. A special interest reflected in allocated time, complemented with other less-demanding work is the most likely arrangement to avoid stress and ensure a balanced perspective.

vii. The existence of the team will have the advantage of building a reservoir of expertise in a difficult area of work. The intention is to foster teamwork and co-ordination of activity without undermining primary professional responsibility or agency function. Such an arrangement would facilitate the development of skills amongst a wider group of people whilst ensuring a reservoir of specialist skill that staff could turn to for assistance with the difficult cases. It should have access to specialist expertise, for example a child psychiatrist or gynaecologist, who would be consulted or brought in on cases of particular difficulty.

c. The following framework and methods of working.

i. The flowchart gives a general outline. It does not cover every possibility. The framework is intended to allow straightforward cases to be dealt with in a straightforward way. It is not suggested that the Specialist Assessment Team deal with all referrals.

ii. All agencies—Police, Social Services, NSPCC, Health, will receive some referrals where there is a clear account of events by a child and/or an admission of guilt by a perpetrator.

— Social Services will receive information or referrals which present a straightforward pattern of information, clear account by a child, admission by a perpetrator and confirmation by a medical examination. Such cases will require Social Services to work closely with the Police and medical colleagues in a planned intervention. Evidence and information will be collated. A case conference will be called to ensure that all relevant information has been gathered and the conference recommendations are considered in the making of the final decisions in relation to civil or criminal proceedings.

— Referrals to doctors are most likely to arise in relation to an injury or disorder. Where an allegation by a child, accompanied by primary medical signs, allows a definitive conclusion to be drawn, the case will need to be referred directly to the Police and/or Social Services. In cases where suspicion is raised by the presence of physical signs without complaints by the child or a third party, a referral should be made to the Specialist Assessment Team for assessment.

— A number of such cases will involve allegations of offences made to the Police by a child or third party relating to events which have taken place outside the family. Such cases will normally be investigated and prosecuted by the Police without the involvement of other agencies. It may be necessary for the Police to draw on the skills of a doctor from the

16

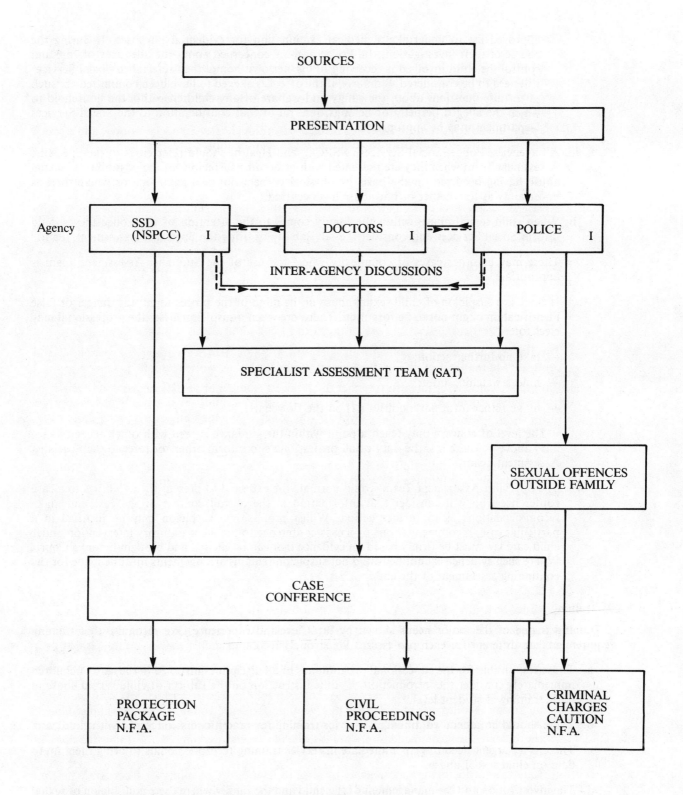

SOURCES

PRESENTATION

Agency
SSD (NSPCC) I

DOCTORS I

POLICE I

INTER-AGENCY DISCUSSIONS

SPECIALIST ASSESSMENT TEAM (SAT)

SEXUAL OFFENCES OUTSIDE FAMILY

CASE CONFERENCE

PROTECTION PACKAGE N.F.A.

CIVIL PROCEEDINGS N.F.A.

CRIMINAL CHARGES CAUTION N.F.A.

I = INFORMAL INQUIRIES   N.F.A. = NO FURTHER ACTION

A FRAMEWORK FOR INTER-AGENCY RESPONSE

approved list to undertake a medical examination for evidential purposes. If during the course of their investigation, the Police become concerned about the adequacy of care and control the child involved is receiving in his/her own home, then referral to Social Services will need to be considered. Similarly, if the offences alleged to have been committed are such as to raise questions about the safety and welfare of any children within the household to which the alleged perpetrator belongs, referral of that consideration to the Social Services Department may be appropriate.

iii. All agencies, Police, Social Services, NSPCC, and Health, should refer cases to the Specialist Assessment Team when they are presented with or become suspicious of the possibility of sexual abuse having occurred on the basis of physical or behavioural signs alone or where there is uncertainty as to whether or not abuse has occurred.

iv. When child sexual abuse within the family comes to the attention of the Police they should inform Social Services and consider the advisability of using the Specialist Assessment Team.

v. There may be other cases of complexity where the use of the Specialist Assessment Team is appropriate.

vi. If there is a suspicion of child sexual abuse in the mind of the professional, the danger of false identification ought not to be forgotten. Therefore when a suspicion arises the professional may elect to:

— take no further action;

— hold a watching brief;

— make futher informal inquiries ([I] on the flowchart).

    The level of concern may reach a point within the guidance agreed with other agencies—see a.iv) above— where it is the duty of all professionals to inform others or refer to the Specialist Assessment Team.

vii. The Specialist Assessment Team would normally be expected to present their findings to a case conference who will consider that information in the overall context of the case and make recommendations as to further action. Whilst professional suspicion may be justified in a particular case, recommendations by a case conference to pursue a statutory intervention under child care law must be firmly based on evidence that can be elicited and brought before a Court. Where such evidence cannot be found but suspicion remains arrangements must be made for the continuing assessment of the child.

9. Training

    Training is one of the major needs shown by the Cleveland experience. We recognise that training requirements are different for each profession. We strongly recommend:

a. Those responsible for the educational programmes of all disciplines involved in the care of children immediately consider the introduction of some instruction on the subject of child sexual abuse in basic training at student level.

b. There should be general continuing in-service training for practitioners concerned with child care.

c. There is an urgent need to give immediate in-service training to professionals to bring them up to date on child sexual abuse.

d. The investigation and the management of the child and the family where there is suspicion of sexual abuse needs considerable professional skill. We recommend specialised training for experienced professionals with immediate responsibility for the children and their families.

    From the evidence presented to the Inquiry there were particular issues which arose and needed to be addressed.

1. There is a need for inter-agency training and recognition of the role of other disciplines. For example police officers and social workers designated to interview children should have joint training in their approach to this task.

2. Police training needs to be developed well beyond the acquisition of knowledge in respect of the criminal offences involved.

3. The medical profession needs to appreciate the legal implications of and their responsibility for the evidential requirements of their work.

4. Those who work in this field must have an empathy with children and 'their feet on the ground'. They must be able to cope with the stress that is experienced by all who deal with these children. It should not be seen as a failure for some to take the sensible course of saying that he/she is not suited to do that sort of work.

5. In a rapidly changing and difficult area there is a need to review and evaluate the effectiveness of the programmes arranged.

6. All lawyers engaged in this type of work including Judges and Magistrates should have a greater awareness of and inform themselves about the nature of child abuse and the management of children subjected to abuse and in particular sexual abuse.

10. **Courts**

We make the following recommendations with regard to court proceedings:

a. Place of Safety Orders

    i. There should be a statutory duty upon the Clerk to the Justices to keep records of all place of safety orders.

    ii. Applications for place of safety orders should normally be made in the first instance to the Juvenile Court during court hours, and only if the court is not sitting or the application cannot be heard within a reasonable time to a single magistrate.

    iii. A simple written explanation of the meaning and effect of a place of safety order should be provided to parents or others served with such an order. This explanation would also be useful for all those who may have the responsibility to care for a child who is the subject of the order. (for example foster parents or nursing officers)

b. Termination of access on an interim care order.

The use of the provisions of section 12B for termination of access and the interpretation of the decision in R v. Bolton Metropolitan Borough Council ex parte B [1985] F.L.R. 343 highlight existing difficulties over access and add urgency to the need to implement the proposals in the White Paper.

c. Consideration should be given to the practice in the Juvenile Courts of attendance of children in court in highly charged cases with members of the press and large numbers of people present. We would urge Magistrates to dispense with the attendance of the child or to arrange to see the child in a private room. It is an appropriate situation to seek the views of the older child as to attendance at court.

The Law on Child Care and Family Services Cm62

We strongly endorse the proposals set out in the White Paper and believe that it is now urgent that they should be implemented. We have considered that paragraphs 45 to 47, and paragraphs 54 to 68 were relevant to the Inquiry. We make the following recommendations on those paragraphs.

Emergency Protection Orders.(paras 45 to 47)

a. A single Magistrate or the court should decide access if a Local Authority sees need to suspend it after an order has been granted on presumption of reasonable access.

b. Extension for 7 days should be in discretion of Magistrates and not restricted to 'exceptional circumstances'.

c. Application for the disclosure of the whereabouts of a child should include the power to commit to prison for refusal to comply.

d. Any dispute over medical examination during an extension of an emergency protection order should be decided by the court.

e. A simple explanatory pamphlet should be published setting out clearly the rights and duties of 'a person with actual custody'.

Juvenile Court

a. Extension of interim care orders should be in the discretion of Magistrates and not limited to 'exceptional circumstances.'

b. A dispute over access on the granting of and during the continuance of an interim care order should be decided by the Magistrates in the Courts.

c. On the granting of a custody order in care proceedings a Local Authority should have the right to make an allowance to the custodian, as in custodianship proceedings.

d. After care proceedings are instituted the Magistrates should have the power to determine, where necessary, interlocutory matters, such as further medical examinations of children for evidential purposes.

Wardship

a. Wardship should continue to play a role in care proceedings.

b. parents should have the right to initiate wardship proceedings, subject to paragraph c below.

c. The President should regulate by Practice Direction the type of cases more fitted to be tried in the High Court.

Family Court

We recognise the considerable procedural advantages of the ability to move cases at any time from one tier of the Court to another, which would be achieved by the setting up of a Family Court.

Guardians ad litem

We are concerned that the independence of the guardian ad litem panel should be demonstrated and, in the absence of other arrangements for the administration of the panel, we commend; the arrangement made between Cleveland Social Services Department and the Childrens Society.

We further recommend:

a. 'Courts should appoint the guardians ad litem. A sufficiently large list of names should be submitted to enable a genuine choice to be made'.

b. An amendment to Rule 14A 6(b) Magistrates Court (Children and Young Persons) Rules 1970 to define more closely the role of the guardian.

c. The Official Solicitor should first be invited to act for the child in wardship proceedings before any other guardian is appointed.

Media, Press and Public

We recommend that there should be rationalisation and clarity in:

a. The right of the press to attend court in the absence of the public. To protect the anonymity of the child concerned, the decision whether any particular proceedings or part of proceedings is to be heard in public should be a decision for the tribunal hearing the proceedings in accordance with the usual procedure adopted in the High Court.

b. The right of the press and media generally to report on and publish information about children the subject of civil proceedings.

c. We strongly recommend automatic protection in all civil child proceedings, whether Juvenile or Domestic jurisdiction of Magistrates Court, County Court, or High Court including, matrimonial, guardianship and wardship; such protection should include a ban on publication of names, addresses, photographs or other identification of any child the subject of such proceedings. [The complete version of the Report contains a draft injunction as appendix K]

d. We recommend wider recognition by the media that the freedom of the press carries responsibility and consideration as to whether in situations such as arose in Cleveland it is in the best interests of a child to be identified.

11. Issues for further consideration

We wish to raise the following matters for further thought and wider discussion, but not by way of specific recommendation.

1. With the emphasis we place on the need to avoid the necessity of removing a child from home, Social Services Departments should consider the appropriateness of using their powers under s.1 of the 1980 Act, designed to prevent the reception of a child into care, to defray for a limited period additional costs incurred by the suspected abuser in leaving home on a temporary basis while initial assessment is completed.

2. Samantha's story given in the complete report leads us to advise that there needs to be more sensitive handling of teenagers who have been sexually abused.

3. There is a need to recognise the problem of adults who disclose abuse they suffered as children and the lack of help generally available.

4. There is a need to recognise the problems of an abuser who may wish to confess to the abuse but is inhibited from so doing by fear of the consequences. Some consideration might be given in certain circumstances to the wider interests of the child and the family and whether different arrangements might be made in suitable cases for those abusers who admit their guilt, who co-operate with the arrangements for the child and who are prepared to submit themselves to a programme of control.

5. We suggest that consideration is given to creating a new Office of Child Protection for use in care proceedings in the Family Court with the following responsibilities:

    a. To scrutinise the application of the Local Authority in care proceedings and ensure that it is well founded.

    b. To call for additional investigation or reports.

    c. To invite the Local Authority or the Police to reconsider the civil or criminal proceedings proposed.

    d. To act as administrator of the guardian ad litem panel.

    e. Further consideration should be given to whether the office holder should;

        (i) direct who should be parties to the care proceedings,

        (ii) direct in which tier of the court it should be heard and

        (iii) have the power to take no further action.

Printed in the United Kingdom for Her Majesty's Stationery Office.
Dd.0500134, 6/88, C180, 51-2329, 5673, 22539.